# COUNTRIES IN OUR WORLD

# RUSSIA
## IN OUR WORLD

*Galya Ransome*

## Smart Apple Media

Published by Smart Apple Media
P.O. Box 3263, Mankato, Minnesota 56002

Printed in the United States of America at Corporate
Graphics, in North Mankato, Minnesota.

Published by arrangement with the Watts Publishing
Group Ltd., London.

Library of Congress Cataloging-in-Publication Data

Ransome, Galya.
  Russia in our world / Galya Ransome.
    p. cm. -- (Countries in our world)
  Includes index.
  Summary: "Describes the economy, government,
and culture of Russia today and discusses Russia's
influence of and relations with the rest of the world"
--Provided by publisher.
  ISBN 978-1-59920-442-0 (library binding)
  1. Russia (Federation)--Juvenile literature. I. Title.
  DK510.23 R37 2011
  947.086--dc22

                              2009043162

Produced by: White-Thomson Publishing Ltd.

**Series consultant:** Rob Bowden
**Editor:** Sonya Newland
**Designer:** Hayley Cove
**Picture researcher:** Amy Sparks

**Picture Credits**
**Corbis:** 12 (Uwe Zucchi/dpa), 13 (Gerd Ludwig),
15 (Thomas Peter/Reuters), 18 (Uwe Zucchi/dpa),
22 (Sergei Ilnitsky/epa), 25 (Reuters), 26 (Ria
Novosti/Kremlin Pool/epa), 28 (Alexander
Natruskin/Reuters); **Fotolia:** 4 (Filtv), 21 (Mikhail
Lukyanov), 29 (Andrey Rakhmatullin); **Photoshot:**
Cover (World Illustrated), 1 (World Illustrated),
9 (Itar - Tass/UPPA); **Shutterstock:** 6 (Suzanne
Bickerdike), 7 (George Spade), 8 (Mostovyi Sergii
Igorevich), 10 (Solodovnikova Elena), 11 (Astrid
Lenz), 14 (Losevsky Pavel), 16 (Khrushchev
Georgy Ivanovich), 17 (Dmitriy Yakovlev), 19
(Paul Cowan), 20 (Gum), 23 (Elen), 24 (Elena
Grigorova); **UN Photo:** 27 (Eskinder Debebe).

1207
32010


9 8 7 6 5 4 3 2 1

# Contents

# Introducing Russia

*Russia is the largest country in the world—about twice the size of the United States. Although Russia covers nearly one-ninth of all the land on Earth, its population density is low. In 2009, just over 140 million people lived in Russia, putting it ninth in the world in terms of population.*

## The USSR

For over 70 years, Russia was the largest part of the world's first communist state, known as the Union of Soviet Socialist Republics (USSR). After the end of World War II in 1945, the USSR and the United States were the two "superpowers" most important in the world in areas such as politics, economy, science, and culture. By the 1980s, however, the different republics of the USSR wanted to rule themselves. In 1991, 15 independent countries were formed. The new country of Russia was left with most of the USSR's land, natural resources, and military power.

▼ *Russia's capital, Moscow, was also the capital of the USSR before the states split into independent nations in 1991.*

Key
■ Capital city
○ Other cities
▲ Mountain

Arctic Ocean

Pacific Ocean

NORWAY
DENMARK
SWEDEN
FINLAND
RUSSIA
St Petersburg
POLAND
ESTONIA
LATVIA
BELARUS
LITHUANIA
Moscow
UKRAINE
Ural Mountains
Volga River
Ob River
S I B E R I A
Lena River
R U S S I A
Yenisey River
Black Sea
Mount Elbrus
Caucasus Mountains
Caspian Sea
GEORGIA
TURKEY
AZERBAIJAN
ARMENIA
TURKMENISTAN
UZBEKISTAN
KAZAKHSTAN
Lake Baikal
CHINA
MONGOLIA
CHINA
NORTH KOREA
Vladivostock
JAPAN
miles  0    500
kilometers  0    500

▲ *Russia spans two continents—Asia and Europe—and it has borders with 14 other countries. This is more than any other country in the world except China, which has the same number of international borders.*

## Difficult Times

After 1991, dramatic changes took place in Russia, and these badly affected the country's economy. By 1995, a quarter of the population was living in poverty, and many people were not being paid their wages. Farming had once been an important industry, but by 1997 it had declined so much that Russia had to import more than one-third of its food from other countries. The Russian government realized that it had to find a way of bringing money into the country, so it turned to its natural resources. The world needed oil, natural gas, coal, and other resources such as minerals and timber, which Russia had and could sell to other countries.

## Quick Recovery

As supplies of oil and natural gas declined in many parts of the world, Russia began exporting these precious fossil fuels. The global demand for such resources helped Russia get back on its feet, and today it has some of the biggest companies and is one of the richest countries in the world. In the last few years, Russia's economy has grown quickly. The global financial crisis that began in 2008 slowed the pace of this growth, but the Russian government was determined to protect its economy.

### IT STARTED HERE

### Space Travel

In the twentieth century, the USSR and the United States both developed technology designed to put humans in space. This became known as the "space race." The USSR won the space race when the Russian cosmonaut Yuri Gagarin became the first man to orbit Earth, in his spacecraft Vostok, on April 12, 1961. This day is still celebrated as a national holiday in Russia.

▶ *This monument in Moscow depicts Yuri Gagarin, the first man to travel in space.*

## Personal Wealth

The standard of living for ordinary people in Russia has also improved. By 2008, most people in Russia were almost twice as well off as they were in 1999, and half of Europe's millionaires were Russian.

## Russia and the World

Today, Russia is the world's major energy supplier. It sells more gas than any other country in the world and is the second largest exporter of oil after Saudi Arabia. Experts believe that there is a lot more oil left in Russia, and this may help keep the Russian economy growing for many years. It also means that Russia has a major influence on other countries, which will rely more and more on Russian oil.

**BASIC DATA**

Official name: **Russian Federation**

Capital: **Moscow**

Size: **6,601,668 sq miles (17,098,242 sq km)**

Population: **140,041,247**

Currency: **Ruble**

▼ *There are already several oil fields in Siberia, in northeast Russia, but experts think there may be much more oil to be exploited in the area.*

# Landscapes and Environment

*Russia spans all the world's climate zones except tropical. It goes from Arctic deserts in the north through forests to grasslands called steppe in the south. There are many long rivers, large lakes, and high mountains in Russia.*

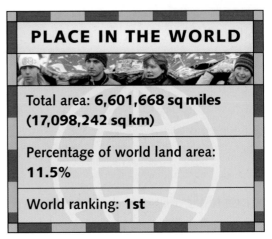

**PLACE IN THE WORLD**

| | |
|---|---|
| Total area: 6,601,668 sq miles (17,098,242 sq km) | |
| Percentage of world land area: 11.5% | |
| World ranking: 1st | |

## Between Europe and Asia

Russia spreads across two continents, Europe and Asia, with the Ural Mountains forming a natural border between the two. This mountain range is 1,500 miles (2,400 km) long and runs from north to south. The Ural Mountains contain all the known chemical elements on Earth, which makes them unique. Many of these elements are very valuable, such as silver, gold, copper, and iron. Russia's other important mountain range, the Caucasus, runs from the Black Sea to the Caspian Sea in the southwest, and contains Russia's highest mountain, Mount Elbrus.

▼ *Mount Elbrus (in the distance) stands at 18,481 ft (5,633 m)—the highest mountain in Russia.*

## IT'S A FACT!

The Caspian Sea, in southwest Russia, is famous for its sturgeon fish. The eggs of this fish are considered to be the best in the world for making the food delicacy caviar. Caviar is very expensive because sturgeon are rare, and the fish must be caught at a certain time so the eggs are just right.

▲ *These fishermen are setting up nets to catch valuable sturgeon fish in the Caspian Sea.*

## "The Wild East"

Russia's "Wild East" is Siberia, an area that stretches from the Ural Mountains to the Pacific Ocean. Siberia's huge, cold landscape makes up almost 75 percent of Russia's land. The coldest temperature ever recorded on Earth, -90°F (-60°C), was in Siberia. This region has large amounts of oil, natural gas, and many precious metals and minerals.

## The Lungs of Europe

Nearly a quarter of the world's remaining forests are in Russia. They are known as "The Lungs of Europe," because they play an important role in the global climate. The amount of carbon dioxide they absorb is second only to the rain forest in the Amazon, South America, and they produce oxygen that is important for the whole planet.

## Rivers and Lakes

Russia has 120,000 rivers longer than 6.2 miles (10 km). The most famous Russian river is the Volga, the longest river in Europe. It flows south for 2,325 miles (3,749 km) into the Caspian Sea. Three of the Siberian rivers—the Ob, Angara, and Lena—are among the longest in the world.

### GLOBAL LEADER

**Lake Baikal**

Lake Baikal is so large that all the rivers on Earth would take an entire year to fill it. It has more water than all of North America's Great Lakes combined. More than 1,700 species of plants and animals live there, and two-thirds of them cannot be found anywhere else in the world.

## The "Pearl of Siberia"

Known as the "Pearl of Siberia," Lake Baikal is one of the largest and most ancient lakes in the world. It is nearly 30 million years old. More than 300 rivers flow into the lake, but only the Angara River runs out of it. There are many other big lakes in Russia. Lake Ladoga in the north is the largest lake in Europe. Lake Onega is the second largest, and is so enormous that it contains 1,369 islands.

▲ *Lake Baikal is the deepest lake in the world, and it contains one-fifth of all the freshwater on Earth's surface.*

## Environmental Problems

Although the USSR faced many environmental problems, these increased when the union collapsed and the new independent countries were formed. Many new industries were started, and there was a great deal of construction. All this caused pollution, and today some Russian cities are among the most polluted places in the world. The Russian government is trying to reduce the environmental damage, but it will take many years to put things right.

## Wildlife in Danger

The lives of many wild animals in Russia are threatened by both habitat loss—the destruction of areas of forest, for example—and illegal hunting for the fur trade. Many nature reserves and national parks were created so that Russia's wild animals could be protected, but this has not always stopped illegal hunting. Siberian tigers have long been hunted for their fur, for example, and by 1940 there were only 40 tigers left in the wild. However, in 1947 the hunting of Siberian tigers was made illegal, and captive breeding programs were later introduced. Today, there are believed to be between 300 and 400 Siberian tigers in the wild.

### IT'S A FACT!

The Neva River, on which Russia's second largest city, Saint Petersburg, is built, is the deepest river in Europe. The river is 79 ft (24 m) deep, and its basin spans a large area of Russia and Finland.

▶ *Conservation efforts in Russia are helping to bring the Siberian tiger back from the brink of extinction.*

# Population and Migration

*People of more than 100 different nationalities live in Russia. More than 80 percent of the population are ethnic Russians. The largest group of non-Russians are the Tartars, who originally came from the area that is now Mongolia.*

## Where Do People Live?

The population of Russia is not spread evenly throughout the country. The European part of Russia and southwest Siberia have an average of 65 people per sq mile (25 per sq km), but about one-third of the country has a population density of less than three people per sq mile (1 per sq km). This includes huge parts of Siberia.

### PLACE IN THE WORLD

Population: **140,041,247** (2009 est.)

Percentage of world total: **2.1%**

World ranking: **9th**

▼ *Saint Petersburg is the third largest city in Europe after Moscow and London, and has a population of around 4.6 million.*

## Shrinking Population

In 2002, 145.8 million people lived in Russia. By the middle of 2009, the population was about 140 million. In the 15 years leading up to 2008, Russia's population fell by about six million—it is the only major industrialized country in the world with such a rapid decrease. Experts believe that the population is now dropping by about one million people every year. Usually this only happens during wartime, but it is not war that is causing the decline in Russia, but rather high death rates and low birth rates. More people die in Russia than are born every year. The world average death rate is nine deaths per 1,000 people every year. In Russia, that rate is 15 per 1,000.

▲ *Russia's shrinking population means there are thousands of "ghost villages," where fewer than 10 people live. Most of these are elderly women.*

### IT'S A FACT!

At 59 years, the life expectancy for men born in Russia is lower than it is in India, Egypt, or Bolivia. Life expectancy for women is much higher at 73. In most countries, women live longer than men, but Russia has the largest difference in life expectancy between men and women in the more developed world.

## Baby Boom

To try to solve the problem of population decline, the Russian government is encouraging people to have more children. Television programs have started to advertise to promote big families. The government has introduced special support for first-time mothers, and it allows women more paid time off when they have children. This campaign has been successful—in the first half of 2008, the birth rate increased by 12 percent.

◀ *A young family eats lunch together during a shopping trip in Moscow. A government program designed to encourage people to have more children is helping to slow Russia's population decline.*

## Russians Return Home

Some people believe that Russia should allow more immigrants to settle there, as many Western countries have done. However, the Russian government does not encourage foreigners. Only people from the countries that were once part of the USSR can easily settle in Russia. During the communist era, thousands of Russians left the country, but since the collapse of the USSR many of them have returned to Russia.

### GOING GLOBAL

It is believed that more than 30 million Russians now live in other countries that were once part of the USSR. The countries with the largest numbers of Russians include Kazakhstan, Latvia, Estonia, and Ukraine, whose ethnic Russian populations are thought to be up to 20 percent of the total.

## Migrant Workers

Although it is difficult for immigrants to move to Russia, the country is still second only to the United States for immigration. Official figures record that around 180,000 migrants go to Russia every year, but the real number might be much higher because many are unregistered. Most of them come from countries of the former USSR. Most low-skilled migrant workers come from Central Asia, and in the east part of the country, migrant workers are mainly Chinese. People are not always welcoming to foreigners, and some blame migrant workers for the increase in crime in Russia's big cities.

## GLOBAL LEADER

### Billionaires

In 2008, the Russian capital, Moscow, overtook New York as the place with the most billionaires in the world. Seventy-four billionaires now live in Moscow, compared to 71 in New York.

▼ *Russia's growing economy means it needs migrant workers to help in important industries like construction.*

# Culture and Lifestyles

*Compared to the rest of Europe, Russia's culture is quite young. Written literature and works of art only began to appear after Russia became a Christian state in the tenth century. Russian culture reached its peak in the nineteenth century, when many writers, poets, artists, and composers created works that are now famous all over the world.*

▼ *A Russian Orthodox procession through the streets of Vladivostok. This form of Christianity is the most widespread in Russia.*

## The Fall and Rise of Religion

After the Russian Revolution of 1917, the rulers of the USSR tried to ban religion. Thousands of churches and monasteries were destroyed, and priests were sent to prison camps or were killed. There was a lot of anti-religious propaganda, especially directed at young people, because the government wanted to be the only influence on the people. Since Russia has become an independent country, religion has become more important, and new churches are being built all the time. The Russian Orthodox Church (a form of Christianity) has the most followers—between 15 and 20 percent of the population.

## IT'S A FACT!

Russia ranks eighth in the world in the list of countries with the most atheists (non-religious people). This is a result of many years of communist rule, when the ruling party restricted religious activity.

## Islam in Russia

Islam is the second most popular religion in Russia. Between 10 and 15 percent of the population are Muslims. Experts think that Islam may become the main religion in Russia by 2050, due to the high birth rate in Muslim areas. Today, there are more than 8,000 mosques in Russia, compared to only 300 in 1991.

### FAMOUS RUSSIAN

*Leo Tolstoy (1828–1910)*

Russian novelist Leo Tolstoy is one of the most famous authors in the world. Two of his books—*War and Peace* and *Anna Karenina*—are included in the list of The 10 Greatest Books of All Time by *Time* magazine, and they have been translated into hundreds of languages.

◀ *The Kul Sharif mosque in Kazan, northwest Russia, is the largest mosque in Europe.*

## Moving to the Cities

During the difficult times after the collapse of the USSR, many people from northern Russia moved to towns and cities in western areas in search of a better life. Today, more than 73 percent of people in Russia live in towns and cities. Many of these cities have grown dramatically in the past 10 years, especially those linked with oil and gas

> ## THE HOME OF...
>
> ### *Matryoshka*
>
> Originally inspired by a Japanese design, the *Matryoshka* nesting dolls—with one doll inside the other—have become a symbol of Russia and are known all over the world.

production. The capital, Moscow, now has a population of more than 10 million.

## Russian Food

A traditional Russian meal has three courses. The first course is usually soup, and Russia has more traditional varieties of soup than any other country. The most famous are *borscht* (beet and cabbage soup) and *shchee* (cabbage soup). The second course is usually meat with vegetables, and the third course is cake served with tea or coffee. Russian food has been influenced by many different countries, particularly France. Many modern Russian dishes have French names, such as vinaigrette, "Napoleon" cake, and "Olivie" salad. Russians like Western-style fast food, too.

◀ *The first McDonald's in Russia opened in 1991. Today there are 233, with more opening every year.*

## Sporting Activities

Sports were very important in the USSR because Soviet leaders believed that winning international competitions improved the image of their country and of Communism. Since then, Russians have continued to excel at sports. In all the Olympic Games put together since 1996, Russia has won more medals than any other country except the United States. Russian women are especially successful in tennis, and players such as Dinara Safina, Elena Dementieva, and Maria Sharapova rank among the best in the world. Russia is also becoming more successful in international soccer, as club teams sign foreign players and the national team is coached by foreign managers.

**FAMOUS RUSSIAN**

### Maria Sharapova (b. 1987)

Maria Sharapova was born in Nyagan, in what was then the USSR. She started playing tennis when she was six, and at the age of 17 she became the first Russian to win Wimbledon.

▶ *In 2008, Maria Sharapova was the No. 1 female tennis player in the world, and the highest-paid female athlete.*

*During the communist era, and for some years after, the standard of living for ordinary people was much lower than in many developed countries. The situation gradually improved, though, and Russia had one of the fastest-growing economies in the world before the global crisis struck in 2008.*

◀ *Large shopping malls like this one in Moscow are a sign of how things have changed in Russia. Although the country was hit hard by the global economic crisis, people still have more money to spend than they did 20 years ago.*

## Life in the New Russia

After the breakup of the USSR, life was very difficult for the people in the new countries. The government could not afford to keep the factories open and there was often no money to pay people's wages. The cost of products rose dramatically, and in 1990, nearly half of the Russian population was living in poverty. In 1991, Russia, Ukraine, and Belarus established the CIS (Commonwealth of Independent States), aimed at supporting each other and introducing reforms to improve the situation in the new countries.

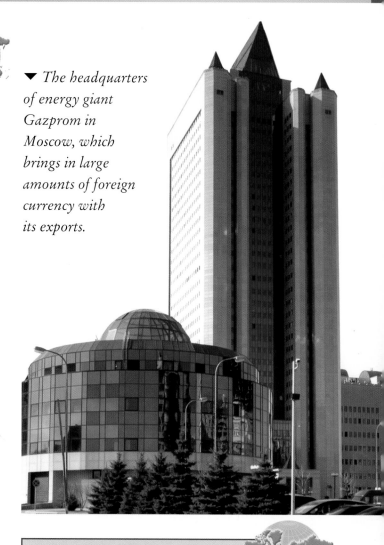

▼ *The headquarters of energy giant Gazprom in Moscow, which brings in large amounts of foreign currency with its exports.*

## GOING GLOBAL

By the end of 2008, Russia was the second largest Internet market in Europe, with more than 40 million Internet users. In Europe, only Germany has a larger online population. It is thought that nearly 43 percent of the population will use the Internet by 2012.

## Plans for Reform

By 1993, 12 of the former Soviet republics had joined the CIS. They all adopted the Russian ruble as their currency, and they planned reforms in trade, finance, and law. Soon, however, the different countries began to disagree. Wars even broke out in some areas, and eventually many republics adopted a more independent way of life.

## Oil and Gas

As the price of oil increased at the beginning of the twenty-first century, Russia realized it could change its fortunes by supplying the world with oil. The economy grew by around seven percent every year for a decade, mainly because of oil and gas exports. Natural resources account for 80 percent of Russia's exports, and about half of Russia's budget comes from gas and oil sales.

## GLOBAL LEADER

### Energy Supply

Gazprom is the largest gas company in the world, and it is a large oil supplier. It provides gas to many European countries, including Estonia, France, Germany, Latvia, and Lithuania. Gazprom also owns the world's longest pipeline, which transports the gas to these countries.

## Economic Crisis

With the global economic crisis in 2008, the growth of Russia's economy began to slow down. At first the government thought that Russia would not be too badly affected by the crisis, but when world oil prices collapsed, the country's economy was severely affected. The drop in global oil prices had a domino effect in other areas, too. For example, with less money from oil, there was less to spend on the armed forces. Unemployment and poverty in Russia also began to rise.

### GLOBAL LEADER

**The Trans-Siberian Railway**

The Trans-Siberian Railway, which runs right across Russia, is the longest railway in the world. It is 5,870 miles (9,446 km) long, and it takes six days to travel from Moscow to Vladivostok.

## Plans for Recovery

The government realized that it needed to expand other industries so it did not rely so much on the income from oil and gas. It began to invest more money in industries like information technology. The government also loaned money to big steel companies and other industries that were struggling because of the crisis. Despite the problems, Russia is still the eighth largest economy in the world.

## The Space Industry

Russia has always been a leader in space technology, and now the country is using its space industry to bring money into the economy. Russia is doing this by promoting "space tourism," where people pay to go on a trip to the International Space Station. This is not a cheap vacation—it costs millions of dollars to take such a trip—but despite this, wealthy people from all over the world, including the U.S., the UK, and Hungary, have booked flights with the Russian Space Agency.

▲ *British-born space tourist Richard Garriott during training for his flight on the Russian Soyuz spacecraft in 2008.*

▲ *A tourist boat on the Volga River in Saratov, southern Russia. Visitors to the country are attracted by the beautiful scenery they can see on cruise trips like this.*

## Tourism

The tourist industry in Russia is still developing. There are not yet enough hotels to cater for lots of foreign tourists, but Russia is a huge country with many tourist attractions, and an increase in the number of visitors to the country has helped the economy grow. People enjoy taking cruises on the Volga River or around Lake Baikal, where it is possible to go bird watching or fishing. Many go to Moscow and other cities to visit the galleries and museums.

### GOING GLOBAL

In 1995, 2.6 million Russians vacationed outside the former USSR. By 2006, nearly three times that number—7.7 million—traveled abroad. The favorite vacation destinations for Russian people are Turkey, China, and Egypt.

# Government and Politics

*Like many countries, including the United States, Australia, and Germany, Russia is a federation. This means it is made up of several regions that have some self-government, but which are united by a central government. There were a number of changes to the Russian political system throughout the twentieth century that brought it to this point.*

▼ *Onlookers watch a military parade in the Red Square in Moscow. During the communist era, such parades were intended to demonstrate Russia's military strength, but today they often commemorate historical events.*

## Total Control

For nearly 400 years, Russia was ruled by a royal family, the Romanovs, who built a large empire that stretched across Europe and Asia. However, in 1918, a group called the Bolsheviks took charge of Russia, overthrowing the government and later killing the royal family. The government had total control over the way the country was run—its economy, education, culture, and even how people lived and thought. Russia's first communist leader, Vladimir Lenin, turned the old Russian Empire into a new communist "super state," which became known as the Union of Soviet Socialist Republics, or USSR.

## The Spread of Communism

After Lenin died in 1924, Joseph Stalin came to power and ruled until his death in 1953. During his time as leader, the USSR became a military and economic superpower to rival the United States. The USSR tried to spread Communism to other countries by giving financial and military support to many countries in Africa, Asia, and South America. It was seen by many as the political leader of nearly half the world.

## Independent Russia

Stalin created a state where people had no freedom at all. No one was allowed to speak out against the government and people could only vote for the Communist Party. Gradually, though, the centrally controlled economy of the USSR began to fail. Starting in 1985 a new leader, Mikhail Gorbachev, tried to introduce changes, but the republics wanted to be free from Soviet rule. In 1991, Russia became independent with its first democratically elected president, Boris Yeltsin.

### FAMOUS RUSSIAN

*Mikhail Gorbachev (b. 1931)*

Mikhail Gorbachev became leader of the USSR in 1985. He introduced reforms that led to the end of Communism and the collapse of the USSR. These included *perestroika* (which means "restructuring") and *glasnost* ("openness"). Gorbachev was awarded the Nobel Peace Prize for the changes he brought to Russia.

▶ *Boris Yeltsin greets huge crowds after he became the first president of an independent Russia.*

## Declining Military Power

As the largest republic in the USSR, Russia had been a powerful military and political force that could rival even the United States, but after it gained independence, Russia lost much of its influence abroad. The Russian government could no longer afford to give money and support to other countries because of all the economic problems and changes it was experiencing at home.

## A New Beginning

Russia's international image began to change when Vladimir Putin became president in 1999. He played a key role in restoring Russia's reputation abroad, but he also restricted media freedom in Russia. Some very rich businessmen, known as oligarchs, tried to challenge the president's power, but they were forced to leave Russia, or were put in prison. In 2008 a new president, Dmitry Medvedev, was elected, but Putin was chosen to be prime minister and many people believe that he still holds the power in Russia.

> ### IT'S A FACT!
>
> In 1991, Chechnya—an oil-rich area in the south of Russia—tried to become independent. Russia sent armed forces to crush any independence movement. Since the September 11, 2001 attacks on the United States, Russia has justified its military action by claiming that Chechen rebel forces are part of a global terror network.

▼ *Former president Vladimir Putin (right) stepped down in 2008, but he was nominated as prime minister by Dmitry Medvedev (left) and remains very powerful.*

## Global Superpower

As Russia became an energy superpower in the twenty-first century, the Russian government began to feel more confident at home and abroad. For example, Russia strongly opposed U.S. military action against Iraq and tried to insist on a peaceful solution. Russia is one of only five permanent members of the United Nations (UN) Security Council. This is the most important part of the UN and is responsible for keeping global peace. This gives Russia great power in world affairs, and its recent growing role as an energy supplier is making it even more powerful.

## GOING GLOBAL

Russia has become the second largest foreign investor among growing markets in other countries. In 2007, Russia invested more than US$12 billion in foreign companies.

▼ *The United Nations Security Council meets to discuss the peacekeeping operation in Sudan in 2009. Russia is one of the five permanent members of the council.*

*Although the Russian economy has boomed over the last 10 years, the financial crisis that began in 2008 has slowed this growth. The drop in oil prices hit the Russian economy badly. Russia may have to look for other ways to keep money coming into the country.*

## A Stable Future?

If Russia's economy continues to develop as it has since 1998, it is likely that by 2020 it will be the richest country in Europe. The government has plans for Russia to become the fifth largest economy in the world by that time—after China, India, Japan, and the United States. It is still hoped that oil and gas will be the main source of income for the economy, as experts think there is still a lot of oil to be discovered, especially in undeveloped regions, such as the Arctic and western Siberia.

▼ *A taste of the future? This photo shows a protest by a political youth movement called Nashi, which campaigns for modernization in Russia but is against foreign interference in Russian affairs.*

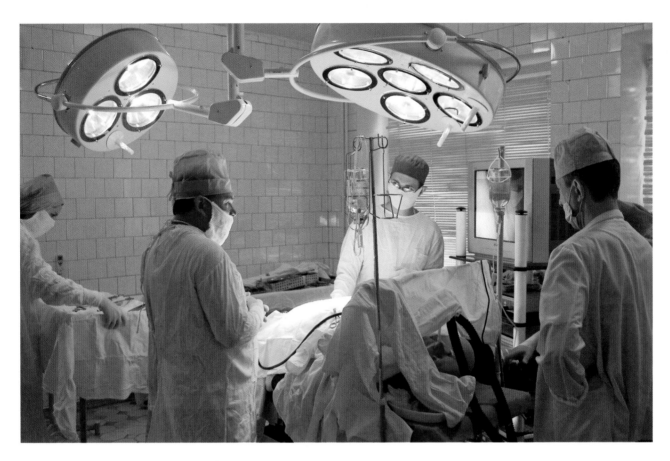

## Future Challenges

Not everything will be easy for Russia in the future, though. There are many problems that have to be tackled, and the health of the population is the most important one. The government will have to invest more in health care and improve life expectancy, especially among men. Overall life expectancy in Russia is lower than it was 50 years ago. If this continues, by 2020 the population will have dropped by another 10 million people, and if this happens, Russia will not be able to maintain its industry, agriculture, or armed forces. Allowing more immigrants into the country may help the population to grow.

▲ *Investing in infrastructures, such as health care, will ensure that Russia's population starts to grow again. Already there are modern hospitals like this in many Russian cities.*

## Russia in the World

Russia needs to resolve disputes with its neighbors and develop a new relationship with the West as a more equal partner. Russia also needs to take a more careful attitude to its environment and the use of its natural resources. However, Russia has made huge progress in the last two decades, and with good government, life for the Russian people will continue to improve.

# Glossary

**Christianity** a religion that follows the teachings of Jesus Christ.

**Communism** the political and social system in countries with a ruling Communist Party, where all property is owned by the state. Food and supplies are given out to the people.

**conservation** looking after the natural environment and wildlife in a country or region.

**cosmonaut** a Russian astronaut.

**economy** the financial system of a country or region, including how much money is made from the production and sale of goods and services.

**ethnic** relating to a specific group of people with the same background.

**export** to transport products or materials abroad for sale or trade.

**extinction** the dying out of a particular species of plant or animal.

**federation** a grouping together of smaller regions to produce a larger political union.

**fossil fuels** fuels (such as coal, natural gas, or oil) formed in the Earth from plant or animal remains.

**habitat** the place where a person, group of people, animal, or plant normally lives or grows.

**immigrant** a person who has moved to another country to live.

**import** to bring in goods or materials from a foreign country for sale.

**Islam** a religion with belief in one god (Allah) and his last prophet, Muhammad.

**minerals** natural rocks that come from the earth.

**oligarch** someone who believes that a small group of people should control the government in their own interests.

**pollution** man-made waste that spoils the environment by getting into the air, ground, and water.

**population density** the number of people living per square mile or square kilometer of a country.

**propaganda** information or ideas that are spread to support a particular view or criticize a different view.

**republic** a political system in which the head of state is not a king or queen, but a president who has been elected by the people.

**resources** things that are available to use, often to help develop a country's industry and economy. Resources could be minerals, workers (labor), or water.

**Socialism** a belief that goods should belong to the community as a whole, rather than to individuals.

# Further Information

## Books

*North and East Asia*
Regions of the World
by Neil Morris
(Heinemann Library, 2008)

*Russia*
Changing World
by Simon Adams
(Smart Apple Media, 2011)

*The Timeworn Urals*
Geography of the World
by Barbara Somervill
(Child's World, 2005)

*The Russian Republics*
Flashpoints
by Simon Adams
(Smart Apple Media, 2006)

*St. Petersburg*
Great Cities of the World
by Andrew Langley
(World Almanac Library, 2006)

*Travel Through Russia*
QEB Travel Through
by Lynn Huggins-Cooper
(QEB, 2007)

## Web Sites

**https://www.cia.gov/library/publications/the-world-factbook/**
United States government (CIA) web site with country profile and statistics.

**http://www.geographia.com/russia/**
Official site of the Russian National Tourist Office, with information about history, art, major cities, and different regions.

**http://www.infoplease.com/ipa/A0107909.html**
General information on Russian geography, history, statistics, and culture.

**http://www.greenpeace.org/russia/en/**
The web site of Greenpeace in Russia, offering information about current environmental and conservation issues.

*Every effort has been made by the publisher to ensure that these web sites contain no inappropriate or offensive material. However, because of the nature of the Internet, it is impossible to guarantee that the contents of these sites will not be altered. We strongly advise that Internet access is supervised by a responsible adult.*

# Index

Numbers in **bold** indicate pictures.